Happy Easter my
darling Chris with loads
of love from Mary xxxx

March 23rd 2008

*To my children
Colin and Clare Louise*

SCOTLAND
Yesterday

C.S. Minto

B.T. Batsford Ltd, London

© C.S. Minto 1970, 1990
First published 1970. Revised and expanded edition 1990.
Originally published as *Victorian and Edwardian Scotland from old photographs*

ISBN 0 7134 6005 9

Typeset by Servis Filmsetting Ltd., Manchester
and printed in Great Britain by
Bath Press, Bath
for the publishers
B.T. Batsford Ltd.
4 Fitzhardinge Street
London W1H 0AH

CONTENTS

ACKNOWLEDGEMENTS

Since the publication in 1970 of *Victorian and Edwardian Scotland from old photographs* several of the individuals and firms thanked therein have died or gone out of business; but the vast majority remain and they are again thanked for the assistance then so generously given.

In this new publication the opportunity has been taken to make use of many photographs which could not be included in the earlier edition. These came, in particular, from the Aberdeen City and University libraries, and Airdrie, Clydebank, Dumfries County, Dundee, Edinburgh, Glasgow, Hamilton, Kilmarnock and Kirkcud-bright County libraries. All are represented in this new publication, as well as fresh contributions from the Batsford collection and the author's file of negatives created between 1965 and 1970. The Yerbury, Balmain and Inglis photographic firms are no longer active.

In addition thanks are due and gratefully acknowledged to the Curator of the Edinburgh Fire Brigade Museum for clearing up knotty points in that field, and the many local history departments up and down Britain that have added so much to this book.

INTRODUCTION

As the sun went down, the scenery became more and more beautiful, the sky crimson, golden-red and blue, and the hills looking purple and lilac, most exquisite, till at length it set, and hues grew softer in the sky and the outline of the hills sharper. I never saw anything so fine.

Queen Victoria: *Leaves from the Journal of Our Life in the Highlands, 1848–61*

This publication came about from a desire to create a reprint with revised or expanded captions to each of the original photographs, in addition to an almost equal number of new photographs not previously printed in the series. Unfortunately, the total number of photographs has had to be reduced owing to the loss of some of the photographs available in 1970 and a desire to improve upon the quality of the photographs overall. The end result is that of the 164 photographs in the current volume, 80 have not been previously published.

In 1970, the starting point in the collection of photographs was the publisher's own file of some 60 photographs, which was added to from a wide variety of sources until it became possible to choose from over 400. The basic qualifications were that every photograph should clearly be of the period from the beginning of photography as evidenced by costume or some other element in the photograph itself, and that all should show daily life in setting or occupation. Some photographs, however, if weak in either feature, were of such obvious merit as to warrant inclusion, and publisher and author were fortunate in arriving at nearly the desired total at the first sorting.

If the selection seems haphazard rather than systematic that is because system can only prevail when the field of choice is both wide and uniform in the coverage of its elements. This is not so with photographs taken over a period of steady, if unspectacular, improvement in the performance of lenses, shutters and negative materials. It was only after the end of the period under review that the great advances in equipment and emulsions were made and it became possible to photograph under almost any condition of lighting, natural or artificial. The uses of flash – magnesium powder or ribbon – were not, of course, unknown before 1900, but interior shots and especially interiors with action were rare; that is why it has not been possible to illustrate anything approaching a fair cross-section of Scotland's varied industries and trades. No Clyde steelworks, no Border woollen mills, not even a brewery at work. Much as these omissions are to be regretted, there is some compensation to be gained from the pictures of outdoor pursuits of many kinds and it is hoped that the sampling on offer will be of interest to home Scots, to folk of Scots descent overseas, to historians and sociologists and to that indefinable entity 'the casual reader' who makes the profession of librarianship so enjoyable and rewarding.

The story of how the Scottish landscape artist and illustrator David Octavius Hill was first drawn to photography has been told many times but will stand repeating. Having been commissioned to paint a commemorative canvas of the solemn and unhappy 'Disruption' of the Church of Scotland in 1843, he entered into partnership with Robert Adamson (who had been instructed in photography at St Andrews by his brother John) in order to obtain likenesses of the many worthy men involved in that religious crisis. Thus came about the most famous collaboration in the annals of photography, but it was destined not to last as Adamson died in 1848 at the early age of 27. Adamson and Hill, whilst working together, used the calotype process which had been invented by W.H. Fox Talbot and had no patent restrictions in Scotland. The process was one where paper was used for both negative and positive image and continued in improved form into the 1850s, by which time the greater speed of operation and clarity of detail possible by the use of glass as a support for the emulsion of the negative rendered the paper process obsolete.

These earlier photographs are again represented in the current edition, though in fewer numbers than in 1970. In this new volume the bulk of the photographs not previously used date from the 1870s to the end of King Edward VII's reign.

The two outstanding landscape photography firms in Scotland in those years were George Washington Wilson (G.W.W.) of Aberdeen and James Valentine (J.V.) of Dundee. Both have left a considerable archive of material. Many of the Wilson negatives are now preserved in Aberdeen University and the Valentine negatives similarly housed and cared for at St Andrews. Much of the output of these two big firms is thus available to current researchers. Many more localized concerns up and down the country are also accessible, including such names as Annan in Glasgow; Burns, Inglis and Balmain in Edinburgh; Ratter in Lerwick; Milne in Aboyne; McIsaac and Riddle in Oban; Young in Burntisland and Bara in Ayr.

EDINBURGH

We walked industriously through the streets, street after street, and, in spite of wet and dirt, were exceedingly delighted. The old town, with its irregular houses, stage above stage, seen as we saw it, in the obscurity of a rainy day, hardly resembles the work of men, it is more like a piling up of rocks, and I cannot attempt to describe what we saw so imperfectly, but must say that, high as my expectations had been raised, the city of Edinburgh far surpassed all expectation. Gladly would we have stayed another day.

Dorothy Wordsworth, 16th September 1803

1. 'The Iron Duke in bronze by Steell'. A view of Edinburgh's North Bridge, c.1885. The tramcar in the foreground traversed the town from north to south and was a favourite with sightseers, as witness the crowded top deck and comparatively empty saloon.

4. West Princes Street Gardens, *c.*1885. The 'Old Town' skyline shows, from right to left, the steeple of the Highland church (Tolbooth St John's), the façade of the Free Church Assembly Hall and the headquarters building of the Bank of Scotland.

2. *top left* The west end of Princes Street, *c.*1905. The prominent churches are St John's (Episcopalian) (*left*) and St Cuthbert's (*right*) the parish church of a great part of the capital's parliamentary burgh. The existing building, 1775, stands on the site of ecclesiastical buildings dating back to the eighth century. Part of the Barracks building of the Castle is seen behind the church's steeple.

3. *bottom left* The Calton Hill from a Daguerreotype photograph of 1844. The Trinity College church in the foreground was soon to be demolished to make way for the southern approaches to the Waverley Station of the North British Railway Company.

5 and 6. The Scott Monument, the most prominent of the statues along the Gardens side of Princes Street, was built to the design of a local architect, George Meikle Kemp, between 1841 and 1846. The two views show the monument as it stood while under construction in 1844 and in the 1880s.

7. The East End of Princes Street, 1859. In the late 1850s G.W. Wilson, the Aberdeen landscape photographer, began to expand his activities and in 1859 paid the first of his many visits to Edinburgh. This is an example of the fruits of that occasion. Note the crinolines.

10. Edinburgh Castle from the Grassmarket. Dated exactly as taken on 17 August 1855, this is an example of calotype (paper-negative) photography taken by the eminent surgeon and amateur photographer Thomas Keith.

8. *top left* Rock House, Calton Stairs. Exceeding a century of continuous use (1843–1945), Rock House must be one of the longest-lasting of photographic studios. This photograph was taken in 1874.

9. *bottom left* The Old Town from Princes Street. This photograph, taken in the early 1870s by Archibald Burns, shows the remarkable clarity of image obtained by the wet-collodion process invented by F. Scott Archer in 1851.

13. John Knox's House, c.1906. Built in 1490 and supposedly occupied by the Reformer in the 1560s, this is the sole remaining example in the Royal Mile of a house with timber-built galleries, once a feature of the High Street. At the road junction immediately east of this point the name of the thoroughfare becomes the Canongate (the Canons' gait or way).

11. *top left* Corner of the West Bow c.1870. The 'Bow' curves up from the Grassmarket, glimpsed in the previous example, to the Lawnmarket near the head of the Royal Mile, which runs from the foot of the Castle Esplanade to Holyrood Palace. St Giles' Cathedral can be seen in the middle distance.

12. *bottom left* The North side of the Lawnmarket, c.1890. The opposite side of the street from that seen in No. 11 shows the older and newer tenement buildings that are characteristic of this and other parts of the Royal Mile.

14. The Canongate Tolbooth, *c.*1890. The separate Burgh of Canongate existed for some seven centuries, being founded by David I in 1128 and only finally absorbed into Edinburgh in 1856. In Scotland a tolbooth is commonly a burgh chambers, a courthouse, a place where tolls are collected, a prison, or any combination of the four. Built in 1591, it is now a museum, part of the City Museum opposite.

15. *top right* The Bakehouse Close, *c.*1905, separating the principal City Museum from Acheson House, now the Scottish Craft Centre. Both contain much of interest to city and visitors alike.

16. *bottom right* Arthur's Seat, *c.*1910. Edinburgh's 'mountain' in the heart of the city, 822 feet in height and volcanic in origin, is at the centre of the King's, or Queen's, Park which includes the Royal Palace of Holyrood House, the monarch's residence in the capital. The park is unrivalled as a viewpoint.

17. *top* Holyrood Palace, Regent Terrace and Calton Hill, *c*.1870. The prominent monuments on the Hill are the National Monument and the Nelson Column in the shape of a telescope. The National Monument, begun in 1822, is all that was built of an intended reproduction of the Parthenon of Athens — an over-ambitious scheme which did not meet the expected support. The photographs on this page are the work of Archibald Burns (see No. 8).

18. Holyrood Palace *c*.1870. The Forecourt and the Fountain. The beginnings of the Salisbury Crags and the Radical Road can be seen on the right with the summit of Arthur's Seat behind.

19. Outing to Cramond, *c.*1904. Cramond, on the River Almond, which forms the western boundary of the city for about three miles upstream, and flows into the Forth at this point, has a long history of its own and was the site of a Roman fort, the foundations of which can still be seen in the grounds of the old church just to the right of this picture. The Riverside Walk is one of the main attractions.

20 and 21. The foreshore at Cramond, c.1910. Some of the attractions referred to above are here displayed. The maltings are on the right in No. 20. A small boat ferry gives access to a path through the Rosebery estates to South Queensferry some five miles to the west. Cramond Island is seen in the background of No. 21.

22. Newhaven Harbour, *c.*1905. Here in 1511 was built the *Great Michael*, of such size that it 'wasted all the woods in Fife except Falkland Wood' in finding timber for its construction. In later times Newhaven became the principal source of seafood for the city.

23. Main Street, Newhaven, *c.*1910. Newhaven and Granton were connected by the Leith Electric Tramways system but the long established horse-bus still made the same journey at this time.

24. Leith Harbour Basin, c.1905. Over the sheds on the left can be seen the harbour and docks office. The Leith Sailors' Home, opened in 1885, occupies the centre background, and the rounded portion of the building on the right was the old Signal Tower. Leith, long a separate town and seaport, was not incorporated into Edinburgh until 1920.

25. Leith, *c*.1905. Old houses in the Kirkgate awaiting demolition. The Kirkgate formed part of the old High Street of the burgh and these houses represented the last remnant of the old sixteenth-century buildings.

26. *top* Portobello Pier, *c*.1910. Portobello is said to have been named by a seaman of Admiral Vernon's who was at the taking of Porto Bello in Panama in 1739. He came to the Figgate Muir in 1742 where he built himself a hut which he named Porto Bello and the name stuck as the watering-place and suburb developed. The pier was demolished in 1917 as part of the war effort.

27. The donkey-ride stand on the sands at Portobello, *c*.1910. The heyday of Portobello as a beach and bathing resort was in the years before the First World War, especially at the times of the Edinburgh and Glasgow annual holidays.

GLASGOW AND THE CLYDE

Glasgow, the chief city of the kingdom next Edinburgh, delightfully situate in a plain and fruitful country is also a perfectly well-built city, divided into four parts by cross streets of a noble width, the houses of stone, most of them five stories high . . . At a corner just where the four prime streets cross, stands the Tolbuith of stone, very lofty: over the jail, in the public hall, are lengths of all the monarchs of Great Britain, but ill performed.

John Loveday: *Diary, 1732*

28. Glasgow Bridge, *c.*1867. On the far bank of the river to the left is the Broomielaw quay from which the Clyde sailings left for destinations such as Greenock, Gourock, Wemyss Bay, Dunoon and Brodick.

29. Municipal buildings, George Square c.1895. The City Chambers form the whole of the west side of the Square, in which the city has concentrated many of its monuments to the famous. These (12 in all) include Queen Victoria, the Prince Consort, Sir Walter Scott, Robert Burns, Sir Robert Peel, James Watt, and two sons of Glasgow, Sir John Moore of Corunna, and Sir Colin Campbell, Lord Clyde.

30. Main Street, Gorbals, 1868. The Gorbals – a once notorious slum area – has now almost entirely been replaced by multi-storey housing.

31. The Gallowgate, 1868. The older shops and houses with crow-stepped gables and dormer windows contrast with the newer housing on the right.

32. The Saltmarket Near Glasgow Cross, 1885. The River Clyde was once famous for its salmon and here was where salt was sold for the curing of the catch.

33. Argyle Street, *c.*1885. Horse-trams were then the means of transport for the citizens and they seem to have been very fully provided. In the 1880s, as today, Argyle Street was one of Glasgow's principal shopping streets.

34. *top right* Yachts on the Clyde, *c.*1890. Yachting on the Clyde enjoyed a boom at the turn of the century that has lasted until today but for the interruptions of two World Wars.

35. *bottom right* Gourock and Gourock Bay, *c.*1880. Gourock was connected with the much larger town of Greenock by a tramway opened in 1873 and was a popular watering-place with Glaswegians.

36. 'Glasgow Fair' Saturday, 1885. The Buchanan Line's *Benmore* leaves the Broomielaw quay for Kilmun, Dunoon, Rothesay and the Kyles of Bute with another 'paddler' of the same line ready to follow. A popular day for a popular excursion 'doon the watter'.

37 and 38. *right* Two of Clydebank's Main supports of the Population. The Singer Sewing Machine workers are shown outside their factory and the workforce of John Brown's Shipyard are seen crossing the bridge over the Forth and Clyde Canal. Both photographs are taken around 1910.

The famous square Singer Clock clock tower, 50 feet on each face and dials 26 feet across, was claimed at one time to be the biggest in the world. The clock's life was a long one – 1884–1963.

39. The Provost of Clydebank on official duties, 1904. This photograph was accompanied by the intriguing caption 'The Provost of Clydebank goes to meet the Shah of Persia in 1882'. Internal evidence, however, does not agree as John Taylor, here seen, held office in 1904. The Dalmuir bus terminus was introduced in the same year and the ladies are certainly sporting the appropriate twentieth-century fashions.

ABERDEEN

We came to Aberdeen on Saturday August 21. On Monday we were invited to the Town Hall, where I had the freedom of the city given me by the Lord Provost. The honour conferred had all the decorations that politeness could add, and, what I am afraid I should not have had to say of any city south of the Tweed, I found no petty officer bowing for a fee. The parchment containing the record of admission is, with the seal appending, fastened to a riband, and worn for one day by the new citizen in his hat.

Samuel Johnson: *Journey to the Western Islands.* 1773

40. Aberdeen Public Library, *c.* 1900. Aberdeen adopted the Public Libraries Act, 1884 and gave immediate effect to its provisions, opening a Reading Room in 1885 and a Lending Library in 1886. The building in the photograph was opened by Mr Andrew Carnegie, who contributed generously to the cost of this and many other public libraries in Scotland.

41. The 'Friday Rag Fair' as seen from the roof of the Town House (county and municipal buildings), *c*.1880. The Town House was begun in 1867 and completed in 1871. It is of local granite, as is much of Aberdeen even to this day, coming for the most part from quarries within the city limits and from further afield in Aberdeenshire, most notably from Kemnay, about 18 miles away.

42. William Bain's Rosemount bus, 1880. The municipal bus service began in 1874 but independent enterprises continued for some years thereafter.

43. Union Street at Silver Street decorated in September 1906 for the quatercentenary celebrations of the University's foundation. The whole town made a great occasion of this important moment in its history and hung out flags, bunting and garlands in profusion. Other glimpses of these are to be seen in Nos. 51, 52 and 54.

44 and 45. Realistic and surrealistic photography, c.1880. George Washington Wilson, the Aberdeen photographer, set up his studios in 1853. In addition to his work in portraiture he later developed a widespread business in landscape photography and this side of his activities is well represented in this volume.

He set up three photographic printing establishments in the city but never revealed how the 'surrealistic' effect was obtained. It is a reasonable guess, however, that it may have arisen spontaneously or could have been encouraged during the use of the wet-collodion process just being replaced about this time by the dry plate. In the older process the negative was coated with an emulsion with a collodion base and the plate used while still wet – the sooner the better.

46. St Nicholas Street, c.1890. This street was among the first city streets to incorporate a tramway track on the inauguration of the service in 1874. Note the watercart in the foreground. These adjuncts to street cleanliness were greatly appreciated, especially by children, in the summer months when prolonged dry spells were a frequent occurrence.

47. The Aberdeen fire brigade, 1875. It was not uncommon for fire brigades to be organized, as in this instance, initially on a voluntary basis. In Aberdeen reorganization as a full-time Town House service took place in 1896.

48. *right* Queen Victoria's jubilee public Holiday, 21 June 1887. The crowds outside the Town House admiring the decorations.

49. *top* Red carpet occasion. Awaiting the arrival of King Edward VII and the royal party for the opening of the centenary extension of Marischal College in 1906.

50. Union Street, looking east, *c.* 1880. The Town and County Bank is on the left with the Town House beyond and Salvation Army Citadel in the distance.

46

51 and 52. More of the 1906 celebrations referred to in Nos 43 and 54. The statue of the Prince Consort seen on the plinth in the centre of No. 51 was later moved to make way for one of King Edward VII in honour of the occasion.

53. The new market hall, Market Street, 1842. The market was burnt down exactly 20 years after its establishment and quickly rebuilt.

54. Detail of two of the individual contributions to the 1906 celebrations illustrated in other views.

DUNDEE

. . . a pleasant large populous city, and well deserves the title of Bonny Dundee, so often given it in discourse as well as in song. As it stands well for trade, so it is one of the best trading towns in Scotland, and that as well in foreign business as in manufacturers and home trade. It has but an indifferent harbour but the Tay is a very large, safe and good road, and there is deep water and very good anchor-hold almost all over it.

Daniel Defoe: *Tour through the Whole Island of Great Britain.* 1724–27

55. A Dundee tram in the High Street, 1902. The first tramway was laid in 1877 and, with electricity as the source of power, the trams kept pace with the growing needs of public transport well into the twentieth century.

56. The High Street, c.1908. The tram on the right has halted in front of the Town Hall (1734) designed by William Adam who, as father of Robert and James, laid the foundations of the Adam style in architecture which continued in vogue for more than a century and a half and set new standards in external and interior decoration. The Ionic pilasters on the façade of the building are an example of the style.

57. The open air greenmarket, 1898. The market was by then, and for many years thereafter, a general market with a wide variety of goods on display, much patronized by the Dundonians and the surrounding country folk.

58. Queen Street, July 1906. Demolition of Powrie's rag, waste and scrap iron store and warehouse was about to begin. The posters promote a very comprehensive variety of beverages to quench Dundee thirsts!

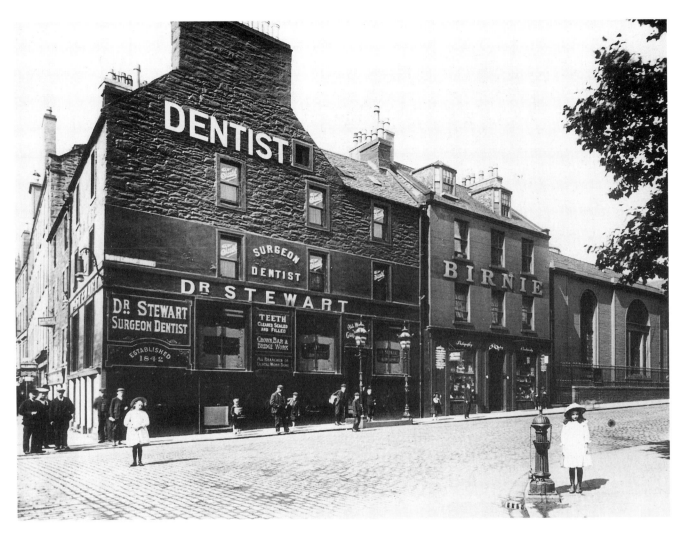

59. South Lindsay Street, *c.*1907. The proprietors of these buildings surely left their prospective customers in no doubt about their missions in life. The young lady on the right, however, had designs only on the services of one of the city's public drinking fountains.

60. The Nethergate looking west, c.1885. An interesting range of shops with hanging signs and statuary to attract attention. Dundee had many 'gates' in its street names. Nearby were the Nethergate, the Murraygate, the Seagate and the Cowgate.

61. The Royal Arch. The Arch was built largely by public subscription in 1853 to commemorate the landing of Queen Victoria at Dundee in 1844. It made an imposing entrance to the dock area. The photograph was taken in 1887, by which time the Arch had become popularly known as the Pigeon's Palace.

62 and 63. *right* The Tay Railway Bridges. In the last twenty years of the nineteenth century no event affected the Scottish public consciousness as much as the Tay Bridge Disaster. On the night of 28 December 1879, after a night of exceptionally high winds and flooding, the high girders at the centre of the bridge gave way as a train crossed the bridge from south to north. No one survived, and the death toll was estimated to be 175. The tragedy aroused national grief and also bitterness as the consequent inquiry revealed that there were faults in the construction and maintenance of the bridge.

A feeling of public revulsion against building the structure on the same site delayed construction plans. By 1881–82 a new bridge on a site well-distanced from the former foundations and on an improved alignment was being advanced. The project gained the approval of the Board of Trade in the spring of 1882, and construction was placed in the hands of Sir William Arrol and Company of Glasgow. The crossing built over the next five years is that which is in use today, having now given more than one hundred years' safe and reliable service.

Photograph No. 62 records the stage of progress reached on the first bridge on March 1876 and No. 63 of the second bridge towards the end of 1886. The official opening of the second bridge took place on 13 June 1887.

64. Beef Can Close in the Overgate, *c.*1900. All such closes and rundown properties in the town came under sentence of removal under the provisions of the Improvement Act of 1871. The Beef Can Close was one of the last survivors.

THE HIGHLANDS AND ISLANDS

Yet even the mountains of Glencoe will not leave me with a more vivid recollection than a solitary sea bird, which while we were sitting on a little rocky knoll, dived into the water just below us and when it emerged shook its wings, turned up its white breast, which actually seemed to flash like silver in the light, and sported so beautifully and so happily that I think few sportsmen could have pulled a trigger to destroy so joyous a creature.

Robert Southey: *Journal of a Tour in Scotland in 1819*

65. Ben More and Glen Dochart, c.1870. There are many 'Ben Mores' in the Highlands and Islands of Scotland (the name simply means 'great mountain'), but this one in Perthshire along with its subsidiary peak of Stob Binnein (Stobinian), just rising on the left of the skyline, form the highest point of the Central Highlands. At 3852 and 3821 feet above sea-level respectively they are the Mecca of young climbers from the central belt of Scotland.

66. Ben Nevis from Corpach, *c.*1890. Ben Nevis, near Fort William, is the highest mountain in Britain, 4406 feet above sea-level. This view gives a more adequate impression of the sheer bulk of the mountain than any other and a visit to the head of Loch Linnhie has proved very popular over the years. Behind the square building in the centre is the spot where the fresh waters of the Caledonian Canal have their first taste of salt.

67. *top right* Oban Bay *c.*1880. Sir Walter Scott visited here in 1814 while engaged in writing *The Lord of the Isles* and his connection with the town is credited with having put Oban on the map. Queen Victoria visited Oban in 1847 and wrote of it in her journal as 'one of the finest spots I have seen'. After these high recommendations there was no looking back. Rapid expansion after the 1850s settled the town as the recognized port for access to the Inner and Outer Hebrides.

68. *bottom right* Castle Bay, Barra, *c.*1910. Barra, or Barray, is one of the smallest, most southerly of the islands of the Outer Hebrides. The castle crowning a small island in the bay was for many years the seat of the Macneils of Barra.

69. Tobermory, Mull, c.1905. Tobermory, (the name means Mary's Well) is situated in a sheltered bay in the north-west corner of Mull, third largest of the Hebridean islands and separated from the Highland mainland by the narrow Sound of Mull.

70. Crofters Stock-taking in Barra, c.1895. Barra, though only some eight miles in length and five in width, will sustain cultivation over a large proportion of its surface and consequently gave sustenance to a substantial number of livestock, principally sheep. The parish also includes eight still smaller islands off its coast.

71. Highland cattle in Skye, c.1900. The long-haired West Highland cattle are well adapted to the harsh environment both in the Western Isles and on the mainland. Herds are small, as in this instance, and occasionally hard to handle.

72. A typical crofter's house interior, *c*.1887. Though the location of this particular house was not divulged by the photographer, James Valentine of Dundee, it was most probably taken in one of the isles of the Hebrides.

73. The St Kilda 'Parliament', 1886. This is one of a series of photographs taken by the Aberdeen photographer George Washington Wilson on his visit to the remote and inhospitable island out in the Atlantic Ocean some 140 miles west of the Scottish mainland. Neither police force nor judiciary were needed to regulate life.

74. Group of St Kilda women, 1886. Life latterly became so difficult on St Kilda that the islanders were evacuated to the mainland in 1928–30.

75. Getting the fulmar, St Kilda, 1886. Seafowl, in this case fulmars and their eggs, with mutton and milk were the staples of the islander's diet. The absence of fish as a staple is accounted for by the fact that it was only in the most favourable weather that a boat could be launched.

76. 'The Hoy Express', c. 1887. Ox cart transport on the Orkney island of Hoy, the largest of the group just south of the 'Mainland'. The house in the background was the island's post office.

77. The Palace of Birsay, Orkney, *c*.1905. The Norsemen knew Birsay as Bergisherad
or the 'hunting territory'. The palace was the home of the Earls of Orkney.

78. Kelp Burning in Orkney, *c*.1888. Kelp is produced by burning the large brown seaweeds, especially the long-stemmed 'tangle of the isles' and bladder-wrack, so plentiful around the Scottish mainland and islands. The weed is first dried in the sun, then heaped in shallow depressions in the sand or on the *machair*, the Gaelic word for the low-lying, often boggy, ground just above normal tide level. The dark grey ash is rich in potash and soda and is used as a crop fertilizer. Bladder-wrack is also used unburnt for the same purpose.

79. *right* Commercial Street, Lerwick, Shetland, *c*.1900. The street, as can been seen, is narrow and winding and paved entirely with stone slabs obtained locally. Wheeled traffic is strictly controlled. Lerwick, the county town of Shetland, is named from the Scandinavian *Leur-Vik* or 'mud bay' and pronounced as two separate syllables, Ler-Wick.

80. Unloading cattle at the steamer pier, Lerwick, c.1905. The rise and fall of the tide is such that there was often no alternative method of unloading livestock.

81. Return from the fishing, Lerwick, c.1905. The scene here is of the Sound of Bressay (a low island seen in the background of the photograph) and the mainland of Shetland. The Sound is some seven miles in length and a mile or more wide, open to both north and south. It offers sheltered anchorages at most points and gives employment for many boats and crews during most of the year.

82. Improvized pony shelter near Lerwick, c.1905. The use of an upturned boat was not uncommon in the islands in the nineteenth century and a few are still in use.

83. Shetland ponies. The ponies were, and are, a small but strong and very hardy breed, for long unique to the islands and the islanders' universal beasts of burden. The thatched building was typically house and shelter combined and some are still to be seen in the more remote islands of the Shetland, or Zetland, group.

NORTH OF THE FORTH

If there are any public works to be executed, which when completed will prove generally beneficial to the country, it is advisable these works should be undertaken at the present time. This would furnish employment for the industrious and valuable part of the people . . . they would by this means be accustomed to labour, they would acquire some capital and the foundations would be laid for future employments. The Caledonian Canal and roads and bridges are of this description and will not only furnish present employment but promise to accomplish improvements in the future welfare of the country.

Thomas Telford: *First Report, 1803*

84. Aberdour Harbour, Fife, *c.*1900. Aberdour, on the north shore of the River Forth, was an important element in the linkage of small ports and resorts that once formed the Forth steamer service. This was based at Granton and Leith on the Edinburgh side of the river. The boat alongside the pier is most probably the Galloway Company's *Lord Aberdour*.

85. The Square, Falkland, Fife, c.1900. Falkland Palace, of which one rounded tower can be seen in the background, had long connections with Scottish royalty and was 'erected', as the legal phraseology of the day had it, into a royal burgh by James II in 1485. Mary, Queen of Scots spent many of her earlier and happier years there.

86. Fishing contest at Loch Leven (Kinross), 1895. The loch attracted royal favour for its especially fine trout as early as 1633 when Charles I passed an Act protecting spawning fish in the many tributary streams. Ninety years later Daniel Defoe, in his *Journey through Scotland*, declared that 'the lake is full of fish particularly the finest trouts in the world'. In the year of the photograph, by which time rod-fishing only for trout was long established, the catch amounted to 14,320 pounds. The historical associations of the loch are legion especially in connection with the brief imprisonment in Loch Leven Castle of Mary, Queen of Scots in 1568.

87. Crail Market Cross, Fife, 1890. Crail, royal and parliamentary burgh in the East Neuk of Fife has a long history, having established seaborne trade with the Netherlands in the ninth century. A royal palace, in which King David I (1124–53) occasionally resided, once stood on a low cliff overlooking the picturesque harbour but little trace of it now remains.

88. The West Port, St Andrews, Fife, c.1887. Though there were at one time five 'ports'; or gates in St Andrews these do not seem to have formed part of a town wall as no trace can be found of such a construction.

89. A visit to St Andrews Cathedral, 1887. The original cathedral was begun in 1161 but not finished until 1318, the work having been carried on by 11 successive bishops. An accidental fire in 1378 caused extensive damage but thereafter all was well until the building fell victim to the Reformation.

90. *below* Victorian coach party at their hotel, 1893. The Royal Jubilee Arms Hotel at Dykehead, Cortachy, near Kirriemuir was a favourite hostelry at the turn of the century for exploring the picturesque Strathmore glens of Isla, Prosen and Clova.

91. Tinker families at Weem, Perthshire, c.1885. The itinerant tinkers, or tinklers — menders of pots, pans and kettles — were generally clean, well-behaved and often to be welcomed when domestic utensils were in need of repair. The typically Scottish dry-stone dyke in the picture was not tinkler work but demanded a special skill in fitting the stones together without mortar.

92. New Scott Street, Perth c.1900. Perth, a city of great historic importance, was, until 1482, commonly regarded as the capital city of the country, and to this day its chief official is titled *Lord* Provost, in common with those of Edinburgh, Glasgow, Aberdeen and Dundee, and enjoys precedence over all but the Lord Provost of Edinburgh.

93. High Street, Kinross, in the late 1860s. Kinross, the county town of the shire of the same name, lies roughly half-way between the Forth and Tay road bridges. It is bordered on the east by Loch Leven, referred to in No. 86. The gentleman – or his ghost? – at the end of the close on the left is evidence of the long exposure necessary in those days.

94. At the High Well, Ben Nevis *c.*1890. Though the highest point of ground in Great Britain, the ascent can be made by an adequate bridle path in about three hours. Here, however, three ladies, with their attendant guides are seen taking time out on the way to the top.

95. Children at play in Broughty Ferry, Dundee, *c.*1909. Broughty Ferry is a resort and fishing port with an excellent sandy beach and a castle (1498) which as now a museum.

97. Scene of the Massacre of Glencoe, *c*.1875. This disgraceful event should never have taken place had not William III, 'King of England, Scotland and Ireland' issued an order 'to put to the sword all Highlanders under 70 years of age' who had not taken an oath of allegiance to him before the end of 1691. Through delays not entirely of his own making, Macdonald of Glencoe was six days late in taking the oath. In the early hours of 13 February 1692 a party of soldiers led by Campbell of Glenlyon, then enjoying the hospitality of the Macdonalds, treacherously turned on their hosts and killed 38 of their number.

96. *left* The Steamer Pier, Loch Katrine, 1875. Loch Katrine, now one of the sources of Glasgow's water supply, is the 'lake' of Sir Walter Scott's long poem '*The Lady of the Lake*':

> High on the south, huge Benvenue
> Down on the lake in masses threw
> Crags, knolls and mounds confusedly hurl'd
> The fragments of an earlier world

100. Inside a Speyside distillery, *c*.1895. A famous salmon river, the Spey is also regarded as Scotland's fastest owing to the height above sea-level of the source and many of its tributaries. On its picturesque course there are many distilleries producing both malt and grain whiskies of the finest quality. The lower reaches nurture freshwater mussels in some quantity.

98. *top left* Feeing Saturday, Arbroath, *c*.1902. Feeing or hiring fairs were traditional in the smaller towns and centres of employment throughout the country. In Arbroath, near Dundee, these were usually on the last Saturdays in January, March, July and November.

99. *bottom left* Benmore House, Strath Eachaig, Argyllshire, *c*.1885. This mansion has long had botanical associations, having been the seat of successive proprietors interested in arboriculture. In 1928, the then owner of the property, Mr G.H. Younger, presented it, along with his extensive private forest, to the Forestry Commission. The whole has now become the Younger Botanic Garden, roughly seven miles north of Dunoon, administered in association with the Royal Botanic Garden, Edinburgh.

101. Inverness Castle and Bridge, *c*.1890. The bridge has since been altered, and concrete and glass have replaced the houses on the right. Only the castle remains.

102. Cottages at Kildonan, Sutherland, 1883. This photograph seems to be concerned with recording the picturesque before its replacement with something more functional. The weighing down of the thatch by heavy stones tied to ropes over the roof of one of the cottages, though by no means unique, has a feeling of despair about it. The contiguous cottage has opted for the addition of material to the ridge and the upper part of the roof.

103. High Street, Inverness, *c*.1880. The Forbes fountain (foreground) has now gone, the figures of Faith, Hope and Charity crowning the Tartan Warehouse have also gone, along with much else that was worth retaining.

104 and 105. The Forth Railway Bridge under construction, c.1889. The need to improve rail travel from Edinburgh to the north was being given prolonged consideration in the 1880s, but the Tay Bridge disaster of 1879 (see No. 62) was fresh in engineering and public memory and in order to allay anxiety a consortium of the top engineers in the field was called together. After much research and deliberation a massive use of the cantilever method was approved and the crossing-point South Queensferry to North Queensferry selected. The photograph, taken by George Washington Wilson of Aberdeen, shows the state of the work in the winter of 1888–9. The figure standing on the wooden jetty at the right gives some idea of the scale of the undertaking.

SOUTH OF THE FORTH

... the lowlands, consisting of alternate hills and valleys, watered by small but beautiful streams, and cultivated with the utmost care, are interspersed with large and busy towns, attesting everywhere the industry of the inhabitants. From the want of complete surveys, its area has been variously computed; but, calculated from 'Arrowsmith's Map' and as given in the report made to the Board of Agriculture, its extent is 30,238 square miles.

J.H. Dawson: *An abridged statistical history of Scotland.* 1853

106. Fountain Square, Linlithgow *c.*1880. Linlithgow, the county town of West Lothian, has an old rhyme attached to it: 'Glasgow for bells, 'Lithgow for wells' and the most conspicuous of these occupies the foreground of this photograph. The site has had a well on it since *c.*1535, but after many repairs the existing structure was erected in replica, or near-replica, of the original in 1807.

107. Haddington, the county town of East Lothian, *c.*1900. The earlier names of the three Lothians were Haddingtonshire, Edinburghshire and Linlithgowshire from the names of the county towns. The photograph shows the main street running west to east with the spire of the town chambers in the centre distance and, over to the right background, the ancient parish church with its windowed square tower, called the 'Lamp of Lothian' because of the distance from which its lights could be seen.

108. Falkirk High Street, *c*.1900. Falkirk has been the scene of two major incidents in Scottish history. In the first, Wallace was defeated at the Battle of Falkirk in 1298 after having had several notable successes against the English in the preceding year. In the second, the account was balanced when Bonnie Prince Charlie routed English dragoons in the course of his return to the Highlands in 1746. The town's modern renown is based on its pre-eminence in the Scottish iron industry in the nineteenth and twentieth centuries.

109. Airdrie Cross, 1904. Airdrie (Gaelic *airde-reidh* – a smooth height) lies on a high point of the old Edinburgh–Glasgow road 11 miles from the latter. Unlike Falkirk, it has no ancient history only coming to notice after 1695 when it is recognized by Act of Parliament as a market town. About a hundred years later it became, with Falkirk, Hamilton, Lanark and Linlithgow, one of the Falkirk Burghs, returning a joint Member of Parliament. The photograph shows one of the first Airdrie to Coatbridge trams. Other links followed although the two towns retained their own municipal organizations.

110. The circus comes to town, *c*.1895. The parade is seen filtering into Mill Street, Airdrie.

111. The Peesweep Inn, Gleniffer, Paisley, c.1890. The 'Braes of Gleniffer' are a range of low hills some three miles south of Paisley that house the town's reservoirs and form a natural, picturesque bit of countryside affording open-air relief for the citizens of Paisley and the nearby south-western suburbs of Glasgow. The local poet and songwriter Robert Tannahill (1774–1810) was much inspired by walking these hills and valleys. One of his best-known songs is 'The Braes of Gleniffer'.

112. Dunn Square, Paisley, c.1905. Paisley, known to the Romans as 'Vanduara', has a long history, including the formation in 1163 of a monastery of the Cluniac order, the Abbey Church of which was razed to the ground in 1307, rebuilt and later extensively vandalized during the Reformation. In the eighteenth century the town became famous for its shawls, silk, muslin and linen and has since developed factories, such as Coats, for the making of thread and cognate products.

113. Colliery Engine, Hamilton. Among the hundreds of books that have appeared in recent years on the age of the steam locomotive little will be found concerning that workhorse of the yard and sidings – the saddle tank shunter. This one, with its driver, fireman, pointsman and yard gangers, seen working about 1910, gave many years of reliable service.

114. 'Black gold' rush. In 1880 surface coal was discovered in the bed of the River Avon near its junction with the Clyde near Hamilton and some easy pickings were to be had for a time. This incident occurred only some ten years after a real gold rush. In 1868–9 gold was found in the drifts of the Helmsdale river in East Sutherland. According to contemporary record 'thousands of people from every part of the kingdom flocked to the newly-found gold field . . . A "city of tents" was erected.' The Duke of Sutherland, through whose estates the Helmsdale ran, tried to organize things and 'claims' were allotted. At first great enthusiasm and harder work brought reasonable rewards but soon the gold got more and more difficult to get, the 'claims' were revoked and at the end of the day it was reckoned that no more than £6000 worth of the precious metal had been recovered. No one got rich!

115. *top left* A day in the park, Moffat, Dumfriesshire, c.1905. Moffat, a holiday and health resort roughly 50 miles from Edinburgh on the former Carlisle road in pleasantly wooded countryside, has the comfort of visitors ever in mind, with a mineral well and a hygropathic establishment among the town's facilities.

116. *bottom left* The High Street, Moffat, c.1905. The street has more the look of a continental square, its proportions (300 yards by 50 yards) not very different from those of Rome's Piazza Navona. The book *The Beauties of Scotland* (1805) described the street as 'wide and spacious, handsomely formed and gravelled, exceedingly smooth, clean and dry in an hour after the heaviest rains . . . and is a most agreeable walk to the inhabitants.'

117. Sheep shearing, Wamphray, Dumfriesshire, c.1900. Wamphray, in the pleasant rolling countryside of Upper Annandale, Dumfriesshire, had a parish population of roughly 500 at the time of this photograph, but it would appear that the farming community could rely on ample cooperation at the times of busy seasonal activities.

118 and 119. The old and new schools, Wamphray. The top picture shows the old village school *c*.1900 and the lower the new public school created towards the end of the nineteenth century to serve a wider area after the smiddy (blacksmith's shop) had found a new and viable use for the vacated, because inadequate, premises. Built with accommodation for 138 pupils, and typical of village school provision in the second half of the nineteenth century, it was, from the evidence of this assembly, perhaps expected to draw its clientele from a wider area. There is a muster of but 21 girls and 18 boys.

120. The Colvin drinking fountain, Moffat, *c.*1905. The fountain, gifted to the town by Mr Colvin of Craigielands, near Beattock, in 1875, may be seen *in situ* in the photograph of the High Street (No. 116). The design has been described as 'somewhat pastoral'. The bronze ram is by the Edinburgh sculptor William Brodie, RSA. The ram is apparently not a portrait but, according to a later writer, 'symbolic of the sheep-farming activities of the district'.

 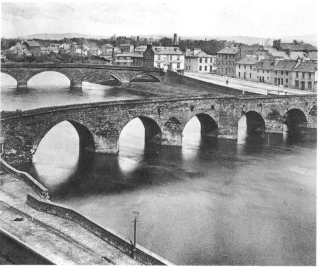

121 and 122. Dumfries, 1870. These two photographs were prepared for viewing in the stereoscope which was then becoming extremely popular. The stereoscope camera took two views of the same subject, each lens of the camera taking the shot from a slightly different angle. When viewed through the two lenses of the stereoscope the images combined to give the illusion of depth. The beginning of 3D vision. The left picture shows the High Street and the right the two bridges over the River Nith.

123. *top right* The High Street, Dumfries, c.1904. It is interesting to compare this photograph with No. 121. The overall increase in traffic is very evident, but the greatest change is to the fountain and its railings. The buildings on the left have also suffered a marked change. Dumfries, the 'Queen of the South' to many of its inhabitants, was dubbed by Robert Burns as 'Maggie by the banks o' the Nith, a dame wi' pride eneuch'.

124. *bottom right* Cattle Market at the Whitesands, Dumfries, c.1905. Originally simply the Sands, on the tidal waters of the River Nith, the area pictured here has been a marketplace since 1659 when the regular Wednesday markets were established. The Whitesands show up as a light open area beyond Devorgilla's Bridge, built in the thirteenth century (see No. 122).

125. Sailing ships at rest in the old harbour at Kirkcudbright, *c.*1895. At this time the estuary of the River Dee was silting up to such an extent that only shallow-draft vessels could use the harbour at all states of the tide. The harbour now forms part of the Town Square. The pronunciation of the town and county name offers some difficulty to the stranger and is generally rendered in three syllables as 'Kir/coo/brie'.

126. *top left* The harbour, Stranraer, *c.*1890. Trading boats are tied up in one part of the large and commodious harbour while another section has a railhead from which a regular ferry service is run to Larne in Northern Ireland. Stranraer lies in Loch Ryan in Wigtownshire, sheltered from the worst of the frequent winds in winter.

127. *bottom left* Cairn Ryan, on the Dumfriesshire shore of Loch Ryan, *c.*1910. The pebbly shore does not encourage bathing but there is a busy yacht club.

103

128. The frozen river Dee in the severe winter of 1895. These conditions were of rare occurrence and stopped access to Kirkcudbright resulting in several shipwrecks in the estuary (see also No. 125). The ruined but still imposing Castle of Kirkcudbright can be seen in the distance.

SOCIAL ACTIVITIES

Now even the poorest labourers take pleasure in the little plots surrounding their homes: the village shops . . . have their windows dressed with engravings of the latest Parisian styles; and the children, barefooted in days of yore, now wear boots and shoes, tacketted and copper toed. In the dead past the only music that ever awakened the echoes of our village was scraped out of the old blind fiddler's instrument of torture, or extracted from that agonising machine – the concertina; but now in all but the poorest houses, you may hear the strumming of little fingers on the keys of a piano.

A.H. Duncan: *Netherton: or, life in a Scottish village.* 1887

129. Returning from market, Shetland, c.1907. The unending social activity: shopping. Note here the woven panniers and ropes.

105

130 **and 131.** Wash day: Highland (c.1895) and Lowland (c.1910). Whether by the stream or the cottage door, the equipment varies little – if you excuse the handily upturned kitchen chair.

132 and 133. Playdays for the old and young. The top photograph shows adults curling at Birnam, Perthshire. Below, children enjoy a day's outing at Cramond Brig, near Edinburgh. Both pictures c.1900.

134. A family picnic by the lochside, 1902. Kettle and the cup that cheers much in evidence.

135. A well-known photograph entitled 'Ancient golfers, Prestwick' c.1875. The Prestwick links are certainly ancient, there being two clubs at this Ayrshire resort even then, but for the golfers the label seems a bit uncharitable.

136. Coach party at The Buccleuch Arms, Moffat, c.1900. Moffat, Dumfriesshire, which also features in Nos. 115 and 116, is still an excellent centre from which to explore not only Dumfries and Galloway but the border areas north of the Cheviot Hills which divide Scotland from England.

137. The Ward Chapel Gynmastic Team, Dundee, c.1900. Gymnastics was but one of the many indoor and outdoor pursuits indulged in in the days before the 'wireless' and the 'telly'.

138. Deer stalking in the 1880s was a serious business – as it still is.

139. The horse class at Weem Agricultural Show, *c.*1900.

140. Four-in-hands at a meet at a Lanarkshire country house, *c.*1907. Not a horseless-carriage in sight.

144. Excursion of the Dundee and East of Scotland Photographic Association, 1882. The excursion was to the Den of Airlie, a picturesque spot in Glenisla some 20 miles north of the city.

141. *top left* 'Old firm' (Celtic and Rangers) Football at Cathkin Park, 1895. The occasion was the Scottish Cup Final, which Celtic in that year won 2–0.

142. *centre left* The first Scotland–England Rugby Union International at Raeburn Place, Edinburgh, in 1871. Only the Scottish team is here (20 a side at that time).

143. *bottom left* Quoits, a quieter sport, 1909. Quoits, a game bearing a passing resemblance to discus throwing but less concerned with distance than with accuracy, was popular in the Borders at this time. The photograph shows Roxburgh Village Quoiting Club with part of their equipment. The method of scoring is not unlike that of bowls.

145. A visit to the Photographer, *c.*1865. The photograph has been taken at Mr Tunny's well-known studio in Edinburgh.

OCCUPATIONS

The manufactures of Scotland . . . are of vast extent and employ an immense number of people. The numerous waterfalls – the abundance of coal and iron, so essential for steam power and for smelting and refining the iron ore – our insular position enabling us to obtain supplies of foreign raw materials on the easiest terms – our climate so peculiarly favourable for all sorts of exertion and enterprise – our skill and dexterity in machine making – have all contributed to the high position occupied by Britain as a manufacturing country.

J.H. Dawson: *An abridged statistical history of Scotland.* 1853

146. Fisher girls, Cromarty, 1905. Cromarty, on the Black Isle promontory to the north of Inverness at the entrance to the Cromarty Firth, lost much of its identity in a boundary revision in 1889 when the former Cromartyshire became part of the newly formed County of Ross and Cromarty.

147. The Aberdeen herring fleet puts to sea, c.1885. Though the centre of the North Sea herring fishing industry lay in and around Wick in Caithness, Aberdeen took a significant share of the catch.

148. Fair Isle fishermen, Shetland, c.1908. The name of the island is taken from the Norse *farr* – a shire. Situated roughly half-way between Orkney and Shetland, its isolation and exposure give little encouragement to 'fair' in the sense of beauty. Life is grim and lonely.

149. East Lothian fisher girls, *c*.1905. Some three hundred miles south of Fair Isle life is very different with a whole hinterland of fertile countryside and a coastline of small harbours from Newhaven to Eyemouth, all of which support fishing fleets of one kind or another.

150. Shoulder net fishing for salmon, 1895. This scene is on the Kirkcudbrightshire Dee, not to be confused with the Aberdeenshire river of the same name. Loch Dee, its source, is contributed to by Loch Ken, which is on record as having harboured a giant pike 7 feet 2 inches long and weighing 72 pounds. The skull was long preserved in Kenmure Castle.

151. Baiting the lines, Stonehaven, *c.*1880. Stonehaven (Steenhive to the natives) lies on the coast 15 miles south of Aberdeen. The success of line fishing, the traditional method of getting fish from the sea, depends on the skill of the baiter as much as of the fisherman – usually the same person.

152. Handloom weaving, Kirriemuir, *c.*1880. Kirriemuir in Angus (Forfarshire) was the birthplace of Sir J.M. Barrie (1860–1937) the dramatist and creator of *Peter Pan*. In his books he nicknamed his village 'Thrums'.

153. Cotton mill at Airdrie, 1907. (Airdrie also features in Nos. 109 and 110.) Unlike wool, the cotton thread is not adaptable to handloom weaving, owing to the shortness of the fibres, and machinery must come into the production of the fabric. The solitude of the handloom gives way to the bustle of the mill.

154. John Brown's fire brigade, *c.*1900. John Brown's Shipyard at Clydebank (see No. 37) built many famous liners for the Cunard company, including the *Mauretania* which established a new record for the Atlantic crossing in 1909 that lasted until 1929.

155. Grand golf tournament by professional players, 1867. Leith Links, Edinburgh, was the venue for this event and most of the famous players of the day took part. Pictured from left to right are: A. Strath, D. Park, J. Anderson, Jamie Dunn, Wm. Dow, Willie Dunn, A. Greig, Tom Morris (multiple Open Championship winner), Tom Morris Jnr, George Morris.

156. 'Rooing' or plucking sheep, *c.*1905. No shears are used in this process. The end-product can be seen, neatly bagged, against the low wall in the background.

157. Threshing corn with flails in a Shetland Barn, 1895. This shows the standard hand method of separating the chaff from the grain prior to winnowing.

158. Bringing in the peats in Shetland, c.1890. The peat-carrying baskets called *keshies* or *kashies* are seen in use here.

159. Making a *kashie* in Shetland, c.1890.

160. Crofter casting peats, Shetland, 1909. This shows how the peat-bog was attacked in layers. Those nearer the surface, being drier, were the earliest to dry in the stacks and were the first to be used for fuel. Later layers were more consolidated, closer in texture, took longer to dry and were often stored separately from the fuel stacks.

161. Quarrying granite in Aberdeenshire, *c*.1890. The scale of the retrieval process is indicated by the tell-tale rows of holes at the edge of the large block. These were drilled for the shot-firers to place their charges, ensuring even splitting into sizes suitable for division into building stone. The guidelines for this later division are to be seen in the immediate foreground.

162. Clay pipe factory in Leith, *c*.1908. William Christie's factory was the last in the Edinburgh area and the workshop has been reconstructed as an exhibit in the Huntly House city museum in the Canongate opposite the Canongate Tolbooth (see No. 14).

163. Merchandising in Airdrie, c.1906. This is a typical small town stationer, newsagent and tobacconist business with the less usual addition of hairdresser. The proprietor, Mr O'Brien, and his daughter and assistant stand in the doorway.

164. Tiring, terraceous, toil. By way of envoy your commentator leaves you with this peep into the way in which things sometimes had to be done in those good old days! This gang's storm-interrupted task was one of clearing a prospective railway cutting near Wick towards the end of the last century.

INDEX